The Key To Our Environment...

COOL, CLEAR WATER

By BOB and IRA SPRING and HARVEY MANNING

Spring, Robert

A Salisbury Press Book by Superior Publishing Company
SEATTLE, WASHINGTON, U.S.A.

Air view of Dabob Bay and Hood Canal. In the distance, Mt. Rainier and Mt. Adams.

Dedicated

to

Dave Brower

and to all other friends of the Earth

working to preserve the oceans and lakes,

the rivers and rains, in a

purity and beauty that can and will sustain the flesh and spirit

of mankind and his companion voyagers

through space.

Senator Henry M. Jackson and a group of boys who are doing something concrete to demonstrate their concern for conservation.

FOREWORD

BY U. S. SENATOR HENRY M. JACKSON

(Senator Jackson, Chairman of the Senate Interior Committee, is the Congressional sponsor of such landmark laws as the National Environmental Policy Act, the Land and Water Conservation Fund Act, the National Trails System Act, the Wild and Scenic Trails System Act, and the Youth Conservation Corp Act. His bills established the North Cascades National Pank, and the Redwood National Park, and the San Juan National Historical Park.)

Man must live with the environmental consequences of his own actions. The proof of this fundamental principle of the interrelationship between man and his surroundings is written large in the landscape of Twentieth Century America. It is only recently, however, that many people have read the message with understanding.

A critical question Americans must face is how to live with the environmental changes that man himself has brought about and the changes man has predicted? We have demonstrated—often to our sorrow—that we have awesome power to effect change. Do we have the wisdom and the capacity to make better choices for the future? I believe we can, depending on how well we design our social institutions, how wisely we write and administer our laws, and how we order our national priorities.

The environmental problems we face in this country are complex. Their history goes back generations and involves all of our public and private institutions as well as our individual life styles. They will not yield to simple answers or to a "demon theory" which finds fault with only a few. We have all contributed to the environmental problems we live with today; we are all individually involved in the task ahead of improving America's future environment.

Fortunately, in the past few years our Nation has made some significant progress towards the development of intelligent long-range public policies on environmental administration; as a people we are in the process of facing up to the question of what will be saved and what will be lost in the tides of social change.

Public demand for a quality environment has already brought about the enactment of needed legislation by both State and Federal governments. The landmark measures enacted by the Federal government over the past eight years include far-reaching air and water pollution control measures; the Land and Water Conservation Fund Act; the Wilderness Act; the Open Space and Green Span Programs; fish and wildlife conservation measures; and many others.

In addition to these general programs, Congress has set aside and preserved a portion of the land, the mountains, the beaches, the rivers and the lakes which comprise our Nation's natural heritage as a legacy for future generations. Since 1960 four new National Parks have been established; eight new National Recreation Areas; nine new National Seashores and Lakeshores; almost one-hundred new Wilderness Areas, National Monuments, and Historic Sites; a system of Wild, Scenic and Recreational Rivers; and a National System of Trails.

These decisions have established in the State of Washington the magnificent North Cascades National Park and Recreation Areas Complex, many new Wilderness areas, the San Juan National Historical Park, the Pacific Crest Trail; and a host of local projects—city parks, boat ramps, and state parks—made possible by revenues from the Federal Land and Water Conservation Fund matched by State funds.

Many of the environmental aspirations and desires of the American people were written into law in the "National Environmental Policy Act." Appropriately it was the first Act of Congress to become law in the decade of the 1970's—a decade which must usher in a new era of environmental awareness. This measure provides a Congressional mandate establishing national goals and policies to guide *all* Federal actions which have an impact on the quality of man's environment. The Act makes concern for environmental values and amenities part of the charter of every agency of the Federal government. It enhances coordination and better planning by establishing new decision-making procedures and by creating an overview agency —a three member Council on Environmental Quality in the Office of the President. The Act also provides for an annual report to the American people on the quality of their environment.

The task of preserving and maintaining a quality environment which will permit all Americans to attain a quality life is still far from complete. Government has not yet fully assumed the mantle of "trustee" for the environment of future generations.

Full implementation of the goals and policies declared by the Environmental Policy Act will require a wide range of new legislative action by local and state government and by the Congress. Priority areas include State and National land use policies; measures to deal with population growth; the development of environmental education programs; increased funding for control, research and development on air, water and solid waste pollution; better methods for assessing the impact of chemicals and new technologies; and the creation of new recreational opportunities.

Just as important as legislative enactments and new policies, however, are the acts and the decisions of individuals to commit themselves to a philosophy of respect and care for the integrity of our natural resources and our environment. The authors of this book have made that commitment. They have strong and sometimes angry views concerning the actions of those agencies, institutions and individuals who, in their view, have fallen short. While I do not find myself in full agreement with their analysis of some specific problems and their assessments of fault, I fully respect and admire the sense of passionate commitment found in this book for preserving and maintaining a quality environment.

Can We Afford To Lose Another Valley?

This book was born in the chambers of the Seattle City Council at a lively hearing on whether or not to raise Ross Dam by 122½ feet.

Make no mistake, both sides of the issue have dedicated men. One can only commend Seattle City Light's superintendent, John Nelson, for seeking to bring the lowest-price electricity to his customers. Equally one can only commend Patrick D. Goldsworthy, president of the North Cascades Conservation Council, for seeking to save our wilderness for all people, forever.

I was very impressed with the various testimonies. The conservationists argued that the higher dam would destroy irreplaceable communities of plants, animals, and fish, and drown the Big Beaver, a lovely valley with beaver ponds, marshes, a tall grove of cedars, and a free-flowing river.

I particularly liked the testimony of one man who said if there were no alternatives to a dam, City Light, instead of spending a quarter of a million dollars a year advocating the use of more power, could advertise conserving power.

City Light, on the other hand, instead of giving details understandable to the layman of why there was no alternative to the dam, hired an expert to testify that there wasn't anything worth saving.

The final straw was a woman who declared, "given any valley with a grove of cedars, Harvey Manning could write an exciting story and Bob and Ira Spring would take beautiful pictures." She did, of course, have a point—but where is there another valley like the Big Beaver? Maybe somewhere in Canada but not in the North Cascades.

Can we afford to lose another valley? By my calculations, there are only seven low-elevation wilderness valleys left in the North Cascades. One, Ruby Creek, will be finally lost to wilderness when the North Cross State Highway opens in 1973. That leaves only six. If Seattle City Light has its way, both the Big Beaver and Thunder Creek valleys will be flooded. That would leave only four valleys untouched by civilization—four, just four, out of all the magnificent wilderness valleys that were our pioneer legacy. Even if the flooding of the Big Beaver were an isolated case, it would be bad enough, but it becomes frightening when you realize this has been happening all over the country.

In the State of Washington, power and irrigation projects have already taken a heavy toll of our mountain valleys, and there are proposals for even more damaging dams. The same is true for Oregon, Idaho, California, and Montana. It is doubtful if there is a state in the Union that hasn't inherited some dam that has done more damage than good.

The City Council hearing went on with more testimony, but I was lost in thought about how much wilderness has been lost in the 20-odd years since Bob and I started our photography career, about how many pictures there are in our file that can never be retaken because the landscape has been radically changed by man.

My parents, who lived in Olympia, often reminisced about trips to beautiful Lake Cushman before it was flooded in 1925 by a Tacoma City Light dam. They bemoaned the loss of the lake, but they lived in an era of "you can't stop progress." They told of a beautiful mountain lake with beaches and a

forest that came down to the shore, dominated by the rugged peaks of Mt. Ellinor and Mt. Washington. They told how they used to hike a couple miles to Cushman Falls, a cascade of water in a narrow cleft surrounded by maidenhair ferns and moss, all shaded by virgin forest.

The dam was only the first of many human depredations on the environment of the North Fork Skokomish River. The 280-foot dam drowned the beaches, leaving steep, unstable banks which even after 45 years are an unsightly mess during the normal 40-50-foot drawdown. In the late 1930s a narrow road was built around the reservoir, going just below Cushman Falls. Though the reward of hiking to the falls was gone, at least people could now view the falls from their cars. In the late 1940s the area was logged, taking away the shade trees, after which the moss and ferns disappeared. However, the cleft was still there and eventually the trees and ferns would grow back. But in the 1950s the road was widened and straightened, and the engineers blasted right through the falls, so now all that is left is a cascade of water over a nondescript cliff of dynamited rock. To complete man's handiwork in the valley, a logging road was carved up the steep cliffs of Mt. Washington to the alpine forest, leaving a scar on the mountain that can be seen from Seattle. Ironically, the ruined lake and wrecked falls are now on one of the entrance roads to Olympic National Park, a "museum of primitive America."

By the time the City Council hearing finished, I was determined to produce a book that would show the conservationists' story of clear, free-flowing water and what we are doing to our environment. When the meeting broke up I arranged with Harvey Manning to write the words to go with our photos and the same afternoon talked to the publisher, Al Salisbury.

One thinks of publishers as businessmen whose main interest is selling books, which naturally they must do or they would soon be out of business. However, I found Al Salisbury has much more than a money interest in this book. It wasn't too many years ago that he used to wander backwaters of the Duwamish River looking for waterfowl in the area that is now Southcenter, Seattle's newest shopping center with 112 acres of buildings and blacktop with an adjoining industrial complex. Ducks are dying by the thousands in his favorite hunting area in Eastern Washington, killed by bacteria that thrive in water polluted by excess fertilizer from nearby farms. Al says that wherever he goes he hears stories from friends of choice hunting grounds lost to "progress."

I was too young to voice my objections to the exploitation and destruction of the old, natural Lake Cushman, but I want to speak out now against continuing plans to exploit and destroy our last remaining wilderness. Let our great-grandchildren exploit these areas if they want, but let us give them a chance. The damsites always will be there, and they can be used 50 or 100 years from now. But if future generations need free-flowing rivers with beaver ponds and tall groves of cedar instead of dams, it could take 500 years to restore the wilderness power companies would destroy.

One can relate what is happening to the environment in other parts of the country to what is happening in our own back yard. There is a similarity to a proposal for nuclear power plants on Lake Champlain in Vermont, Lake Cayuga in New

York, to the power plant on Puget Sound, for none have had a thorough study of the effects of heat pollutants on their waters. A road across the Great Smoky Mountains National Park is similar to a proposal to cut the Olympic National Park in two. Subdivisions on the side of Mauna Loa will be death to Hawaiian wildlands as surely as subdivisions have spelled the end of public use of many streams and lakes around our own home. Miners are threatening the White Cloud Mountains in Idaho with an open pit mine, an area that outdoors people say is as beautiful as Image Lake in our Washington, also being threatened by a similar mine. Even the pulp mill polluting Lake Baikal in Siberia has a familiar sound.

Lake Champlain is only a name in my history book. I never heard of Lake Cayuga before irate citizens protested the power plant. I have never been to the Great Smoky Mountains and Lake Baikal, but I have a feeling they too are worth saving. Thank goodness there are enough concerned citizens across our country, and in faraway Russia, who are willing to stand up and be heard so at least some of the places will be saved for our great-grandchildren to enjoy.

What we have done to water isn't all bad. The story of good works accomplished and landmark legislation achieved are told by the Honorable Henry M. Jackson, Washington's senator. Senator Jackson fought to preserve our environment long before it was a popular subject. Two of his most notable contributions were steering the North Cascades and Redwoods National Parks bills through Congress and, more recently, his outstanding work on the National Environmental Policy Act.

Experiences with water are very personal. We have written about and photographed our home waters, those we know best, and haven't tried to cover all the water of the Northwest, or the world. We offer our experiences to stimulate people to think of their own home waters, wherever they may be, to see their beauties, and dangers, and to reminisce how many of their favorite haunts have been lost to progress.

JUNE 1970   IRA SPRING

Toleak Point, Olympic National Park.

TABLE OF CONTENTS

Cushman "Lake" (a fluctuating reservoir). In distance, Mt. Ellinor left, Mt. Washington right. A logging road now scars the forested hills beneath the summits.

CHAPTER I

SKY WATER
...the ocean is the beginning

Winter storms pummel the coast with gale-driven torrents. Summer sea mists seep through rain forests, feeding lush mosses draping branches of hemlock and spruce and maple.

Rising to cross the Olympic Mountains, ocean-soaked winds dump as much as 16 feet of water a year on west slopes.

Then air masses descend into Puget Sound country, where annual precipitation dwindles to 3 or 4 feet, and in some spots to little more than a foot. Most of the sky water comes in winter, but in every season there are drizzles, fogs, and low stratus.

So near the Pacific, even sunshine makes clouds; after a warm-to-hot summer day or two, usually the familiar on-shore flow commences, drawing a blanket of ocean gray across the lowlands—while mountains stand free and bright.

Other summer days, though, unstable air masses do nothing worse to lowland skies than add decorations of amiable white billows, yet condense on the mountains into "good weather clouds"—mists filtering through high forests and drifting over meadows—rains pitter-pattering on campers' tents and freshening alpine grass and flowers.

Beyond Puget Sound the air masses rise for a second mountain passage, and enough water remains to drench west slopes of the Cascades as thoroughly as the Olympics.

The Cascade Crest divides two distinct geographic provinces. Sometimes sea fogs fill western valleys to the crest, spill over passes—and instantly melt to nothing. Often a "good weather rain" falls for days on the crest—and eastward a mile or two is the edge of blue. Even the storms are drier beyond the crest; a Puget Sound cloudburst may become, on the Columbia Plateau, a loud wind raising dust devils from the sagebrush, rolling tumbleweed over the fields and down the roads.

At the far, Idaho border of the plateau, mountains again force the air masses upward and again clouds form.

The east-sider, child of sun and the big sky, gets claustrophobia in drizzles on the ocean slope of the Cascades, under the sheet of gray. He worries about rust invading his joints and mould infesting his skin.

The west-sider grows restless in sun country. The novelty of day-after-day blueness is interesting, but soon boredom builds and a sense of estrangement. He yearns for the busy sky of home.

Many a time our Manning family gang has camped in a cloud-washed alpine meadow and prowled flowers and trees and creeks and rocks, minutely examining fine details of our limited world, hoping for the sun to burn away clouds hiding the horizons.

We also remember backpacking to Lake Ann during a rare spell of clear and windless weather. We planned to spend a week in the gardens beneath the wall of Mount Shuksan, but after several days of punishing sun, being baked from sleeping bags soon after dawn, hiding from the overhead fire in boulder shadows, tossing cups of water at each other to prevent dessication, our west-side gang evacuated the disaster area of the sun-struck Cascades and escaped to Rialto Beach—and how blessed it was to walk beside the surf in soft and cool mists from the sea.

There is endless activity and variety in the Northwest sky as ocean winds bring nourishment to forests and glaciers, flowers and rivers. To know the land one must walk in the sun. But also one must wander within a cloud, wrapped in the gray privacy and isolation of sky water meeting the earth.

Cumulus cloud above Kalaloch Beach—water in the sky, water in the sea.

Nisqually River and Ricksecker Point.

Elk Pass, near Randle.

Mt. Maxwell, on Salt Spring Island, British Columbia.

Spirit Lake, Idaho.

Lenticular cloud on lee side of Mt. Rainier, signaling the approach of a moist air mass from the Pacific Ocean—and perhaps a storm tomorrow.

Page 20. Raindrops on lupine. Stehekin Valley, North Cascades National Park.

Page 21. Tiger lily in the rain. Stehekin Valley.

Fog drifting through the trees around Three Lakes, Mt. Rainier National Park.

Rainy day at Naches Pass.

Air view of North Fork Stillaguamish River, near Oso.

Rain squall from Chopaka Mountain, at the east edge of the North Cascades. Relatively little sky water penetrates to this Okanogan country, protected from ocean storms by range upon range to the west.

Morning mist in the rain forest of the Hoh River, Olympic National Park.

Burley Mountain, near Randle.

CHAPTER II

SNOW WATER

At sea level in the Northwest, snow is so uncommon that a few sloppy flakes of slush paralyze traffic and close schools and send the kids off on a holiday celebration. A short distance away, though, a mile above the sea in the Olympics and Cascades, the entire year is snow season.

Weeks before calendar summer ends, the first winter-type storm sweeps the mountains; afterward, when the sun returns, hikers pick ripe blueberries amid white crystals of September.

Crystals melt, the low October sun ignites flames of fall color, then another cold storm, sunshine again, and now hikers roam straw-yellow grass and wine-red berry bushes poking through the snow.

More storms, more frequent, November snows bury the meadows, and skiers and snowshoers replace the hikers.

Deeper and yet deeper the snows of December, January, and February heap, and lower creeps the whiteness into mountain valleys—occasionally to saltwater beaches.

Comes March and the snowline retreats upward—but again to contradict the calendar, the start of spring is also generally the time of maximum snow accumulation on high, usually 13 feet or more and occasionally 25 or 30 feet.

The mountain winter lasts far into calendar spring, yet in April and May the snowpack thins, though the surface is frequently freshened by new flakes. Flowers blossom on valley floors; up high, rocky knolls melt free amid the white world and creeks and rivers grow larger and louder.

June is torrents and whiteness—and color. Snowfields that seemed eternal vanish by solar magic, instantaneously replaced by fields of green shoots and bright blossoms.

In the high summer of July and August the grass and flowers encroach on shrinking islands of white—while now and then new snow and frost touch up the greenery, quickly shaken off in following sunshine but reminding that September is near.

Every month is snow time in Northwest hills. And despite mobs at ski resorts and racketing snowmobiles on valley roads, most of the snow in most of the mountains offers a kind of solitude increasingly rare.

On a dark December day, drive a mountain road as far as cars can go and walk the forest amid big white flakes floating between green branches. Lonely, calm, and quiet.

Ski away from the tow hill, over a ridge beyond reach of loudspeaker yodels. Feel the purity of a landscape once more virgin, find in the symbol of snow the hope of a clean earth.

In cold and rocky corners of Northwest mountains the snow from one winter often outlasts the succeeding summer. During a cycle of cool years the snowfields become "permanent." More cool years and they broaden and thicken and glaciers are born.

Of the 990 identified glaciers in the United States south of Alaska, 674—and 77 percent of the total glacier area—are in the Cascades and Olympics of Washington. Admittedly, all this is merely a heavy frost compared to the Greenland icecap, but Northwest glaciers lie in an unusual context of forests and flowers. It's friendly ice.

I recall the first time my daughters walked on a glacier. We'd climbed from White Chuck River forests to the gardens of Pumice Creek cirque. At the saddle above the cirque, right next to blossoms of moss campion and yellow heather, was the margin of the Ptarmigan Glacier. Crevasses began barely a dozen yards away. I allowed the girls to step a few safe feet outward from the flowers—and how full of awe they were to stand on the living ice that had sculptured the mountain world.

Not all glaciers are easy. I remember a January twilight beside the Blue Glacier of Mount Olympus, the summit lost in clouds steadily lowering, the first snowflakes melting on our cheeks, gusts of ice wind flapping our parkas. We three were 18 miles by snowshoe from the end of the Hoh River road and the nearest other humans. The building storm would keep us from our goal, the summit of Olympus, and would make problems in retreating those 18 miles homeward, and there would be no help from anyone if the problems were too tough. What a solemn place, like a cathedral. What a happy-crazy, lonely-wild time—absolutely free in winter snow.

Heather Meadows, Mt. Baker.

Sunrise on Mt. Rainier, from Mazama Ridge.

Frosted alpine trees on a ridge of Mt. Baker.

Mt. Baker from Kulshan Ridge.

Icicles near Rainbow Falls, in the Stehekin Valley of the Lake Chelan
National Recreation Area.

Stehekin, at the head of Lake Chelan. Note the snow-covered mudflats and stumps where formerly the Stehekin River meandered into the lake, until a dam was built at the town of Chelan, 50 miles away, raising the water level by 20 feet and drowning forests and marshes. In summer the lake is high and the ugliness hidden—but not forgotten by those who mourn the loss of the natural, beautiful inlet area.

Oakland Bay, near Shelton.

Coltsfoot pushing through snow on Carbon Ridge.

Coyote track near Stehekin.

Stehekin River, North Cascades National Park.

Early morning view from Camp Muir, 10,000 feet high on Mt. Rainier, looking east across the Cowlitz Glacier.

Sunset from Camp Muir on Mt. Rainier. Eagle Peak, in the Tatoosh Range, surrounded by clouds. In the distance, Mt. St. Helens.

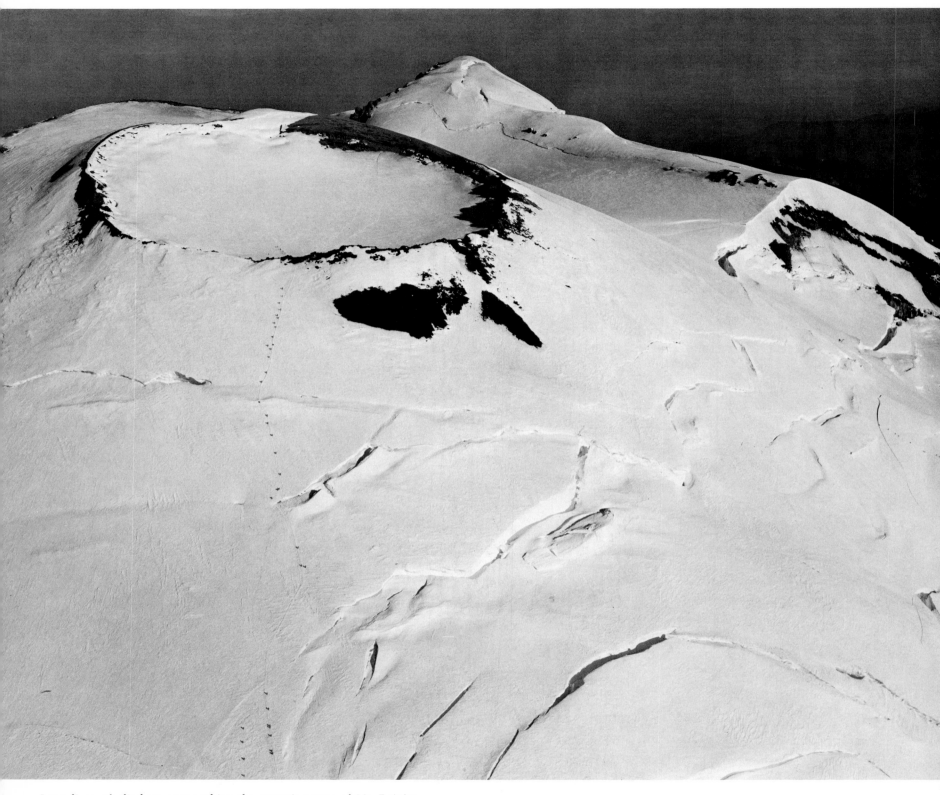

Long lines of climbers approaching the summit crater of Mt. Rainier.
The far rim of the crater is Columbia Crest, highest of the mountain's
three peaks. Beyond is another of the peaks, Liberty Cap.

Ten Peak Mountain and a glacier on Clark Mountain, Glacier Peak Wilderness Area.

Air view of Mt. Rainier, with Camp Muir in foreground and the Cowlitz
Glacier, Ingraham Glacier, and Little Tahoma beyond.

Blue Glacier on Mt. Olympus.

Climbers on the Blue Glacier, nearing the summit of Mt. Olympus.

Snowfield Peak and Neve Glacier, North Cascades National Park.

Exploring a crevasse on the Ingraham Glacier of Mt. Rainier.

Climbing an ice serac on the Ingraham Glacier, Mt. Rainier.

Icicles hanging from a tilted serac on the Ingraham Glacier. Little Tahoma in distance. Mt. Rainier National Park.

Paradise Ice Cave, Mt. Rainier National Park.

Page 52. Lou Whittaker climbing out of a crevasse in the Cowlitz Glacier of Mt. Rainier.

Page 53. Rainbow Falls in the Stehekin Valley, Lake Chelan National Recreation Area.

CHAPTER III

MOUNTAIN WATER

Winter is the season of storing mountain water in snow crystals. Spring and summer unlock the hoard and send the water tumbling back to the sea.

Waterfalls from hanging glaciers foam down cliffs. Icy streams pour from caves under valley glaciers and brawl amid morainal boulders. Trickles and gushes from snowfields run cold and clear across greening meadows, splash wildly over boulders. Little creeks join to form big creeks, big creeks unite in rivers pounding through gorges, roaring between ranks of tall trees.

Mountain memories are full of water. On a hot July day our family bunch hiked the steep trail from Monte Cristo to Glacier Basin, pulled off boots, and explored snowfed creeks barefoot, wading along bright sand and pebbles, now and then stepping onto banks of blossoms while sensation returned to tingling toes.

On a sweltering August day we hauled heavy packs up the Little Wenatchee River trail, the switchbacks endless and dry, our mouths sticky as glue, clouds of flies tormenting every step. Then the way leveled out in Meander Meadow, and a deep, slow stream wound under overhanging banks of lush grass, and we dropped packs, tore off boots and clothes, and fled from sun and flies by diving into cool-delicious water. Not until shadows sent the bugs to bed did we emerge into flowers.

Because Northwest mountains once were even richer in ice than now, they are richer than ever in lakes. Existing glaciers pluck slowly at nurturing peaks. Formerly they were larger and more numerous and vigorous and scooped out the sides of mountains and widened and deepened valleys. As the ice melted, water filled the holes, making cirque lakes on high, trough lakes down low. A devout worshipper of ice would call the present extent of Northwest glaciers a pitiful remnant of past glory. But lake lovers can defend the present era. In Washington alone, 3813 lakes have been counted; a relatively few are fake lakes (man-dammed reservoirs), others are the results of landslides or other natural causes, but most are in one way or another the legacy of ice. Thousands are mountain lakes filling alpine cirques or the channels of valley glaciers.

Some are very old—such as Lake Chelan, which dates to the Pleistocene. Some are very new—such as Perfect Lake, in a raw morainal waste that 20 years ago was beneath the Challenger Glacier.

There are big lakes and tiny ponds, deep blue lakes rimmed by cliffs and shallow lakes amid meadows, and one-time lakes now become reedy marshes or grassy fields. So various are the depths and sizes and elevations, and the settings under rugged peaks or on the sides of gentle ridges, and the surroundings of forest or rockslide or snowfield or cliff or garden, any catalogue of alpine lakes would have to be broken into several families and scores of species—and every lake, though it may resemble others, is individual and unique.

Last summer our family backpacked to Lake Byrne, across the White Chuck River from Glacier Peak, a superb example of the large, deep, blue, cliff-ringed species and long famous among fishermen. Over the ridge I found another sort of lake —nameless and fameless, small and shallow, bordered around by flats of grass and moss. One morning (knowing what would happen, and thus happy with anticipation) I led my 9-year-old daughter and 5-year-old son to the ridge crest; they looked down to the sun-sparkling water and whooped and hollered.

They named themselves "The Turtles" and waded the tiny inlet stream rippling over bright sands between moss banks, and waded from green shores to rock islands, and ran splashing along the bottom of slippery, ice-milled silt, stopping short and skidding and falling in explosions of spray and squeals. For variety they dammed the inlet creek and gleefully watched the barrier of sand be torn away in a flood, and fought wars with Daddy armed with cups of water. Afternoon shadows cooled the basin and we hiked back to camp beside Lake Byrne—and returned next day for another morning-to-evening romp. They wanted to build a house at "Turtle Lake" and live there forever. And I would have except it's a long commute to the city. But for two days the lake was their home and mine and in part always will be.

Cub Lake and Dome Peak, Glacier Peak Wilderness Area.

Napeequa River from Little Giant Pass, Glacier Peak Wilderness Area.

Larch Lake, near Leavenworth.

Marsh marigolds and the Paradise River, Mt. Rainier National Park.

Comet Falls, Mt. Rainier National Park.

Image Lake and Glacier Peak, the Suiattle River valley in between.

Mt. Rainier from Eunice Lake.

61

Martha Falls on the Wonderland Trail of Mt. Rainier National Park.

Reflecting pool on Faraway Rock; Mt. Rainier National Park. Tatoosh Range in distance.

Devil Peak and Mirror Lake in the Seven Devils Range, Idaho.

Stanley Lake and McGowan Peak, Idaho.

Paradise Valley, Mt. Rainier National Park.

Image Lake and Glacier Peak. The surroundings of this classic and famous lake are in jeopardy from Kennecott Copper Corporation's proposed open pit copper mine on nearby Plummer Mountain.

Fish Lake, near Salmon la Sac.

Lightning Creek footbridge and Ross "Lake," actually a fluctuating reservoir. During winter and spring, Seattle City Light lowers the water level drastically, exposing mud-crusted cliffs, wastelands of muck, and miles of stumps.

Big Beaver Valley, the lower 6 miles of which will be drowned if Seattle
City Light raises Ross Dam, as it proposes to do.

Thunder Creek trail, which will be flooded if Seattle City Light proceeds
with plans to build a dam in this valley.

Packwood Lake and Johnson Peak. Since this picture was taken in 1958, the lovely lake has been tapped for a tiny amount of peaking power. Despite assurance by PUD "experts" that nothing would be disturbed, the small dam at the outlet was accidentally built 10 feet higher than intended. Uncontrollable fluctuation of the water level has killed trees and shrubs along the shore.

Waterfall flowing into Boulder Creek, near Darrington.

CHAPTER IV

LOWLAND WATER

From glaciers and snowfields and alpine lakes, from mountain meadows and forests, dribbles gather into torrents, creeks into rivers.

The sky waters and mountain waters build mighty rivers: the Columbia, "River of the West," which drains portions of five states and two provinces; the Snake, tributary to the Columbia but no less majestic for that; the Skagit, master stream of the west slope of the North Cascades, flowing from British Columbia to Puget Sound.

The sky-and-high waters also build short rivers that run down the east and south slopes of the Cascades into the Columbia and down the west slope into Puget Sound, and down all slopes of the Olympics to saltwater, steep rivers that begin as white rapids, then move wider and slower over the plains.

Listen to the magic of the Indian past: Okanogan and Similkameen and Sinlahekin, Pasayten and Chewack, Methow and Twisp and Stehekin and Entiat, Chiwawa and Wenatchee, Teanaway and Cle Elum and Yakima, Naches and Klickitat, Toutle and Kalawa and Cispus and Cowlitz, Nisqually and Puyallup and Duwamish, Snoqualmie and Tolt and Skykomish and Snohomish and Stillaguamish, Suiattle and Sauk and Skagit, Nooksack and Chilliwack, Skokomish and Hamma Hamma and Duckabush and Dosewallips and Quilcene, Elwha and Pysht, Soleduc and Bogachiel and Hoh and Queets and Quinault, Humptulips and Hoquiam and Wishkah and Wynoochee and Satsop. And find poetry in White and Green, White Chuck and Greenwater, Early Winters and Icicle, Lost and Bumping and Wind, Cedar and Carbon and Cascade.

Fishermen feel the magic and the poetry, casting for trout in summer or steelhead in winter, walking the banks on foot or drifting downstream in boats.

And canoeists and kayakers, too. I recall a winter day floating along the Snoqualmie River above Fall City, rounding a bend and being startled by a rugged peak rising high above the tree-lined avenue of water. What strange mountain was this? For a moment I was disoriented and excited, as if the river had carried us to an unknown land, until I recognized familiar Mount Si; for an instant I'd seen old Si with the eyes of the Indians and pioneers—a wilderness mountain. We were riding the river through an area of farms and sawmills and towns, but civilization was screened by trees and the year could have been 1850—or 1492 or 1066, for all that.

The Northwest is the only part of the nation offering so many opportunities for river sport in every season, so wide a range from experts-only slaloms down turbulent rapids to easy-and-serene drifting for novices. River-running is sure to become as popular in the Northwest someday as skiing is now.

There are mountain-born rivers by the score—and humbler lowland creeks by the hundreds, fed by rains on foothill forests, winding by pastures and suburbs and towns. Streams for fishing, streams for wading and birdwatching and thinking, and streams making music to live by.

Our home creek on Cougar Mountain flows only after heavy winter rains. It has started as early as October and lasted as late as May but ordinarily we enjoy the sound of water (plus frogs in season) less than half the year. Even so unpretentious a creek has a potential for drama. After a cloudburst in the night we may hear in our sleep a modest thunder that stirs dreams of high hills and in morning behold our driveway and yard inches deep in a reckless rush of wild water. Some people would organize a flood control district and build storm drains. We feel lucky to be reminded, though only occasionally, of the connection between the sky and the sea, and our place in between.

When glaciers melted from Puget Sound lowlands they left an infant landscape, disorganized and undrained and pocked with lakes. Each is geologically temporary—inlet streams dump loads of sand, gravel, and mud, seeking to fill the lake; outlet streams cut downward, seeking to drain the lake; plants push outward from the shore and algae cover the surface. Nature abhors lakes and works steadily to convert them into marshes, peat bogs, and ultimately dry land. Only when all lakes are gone is the landscape "mature" in the terminology of geomorphologists.

Man has come to Puget Sound at a point in time when the lowland region is mostly young and lakes are abundant. And man does not abhor lakes—or bird-busy marshes and peat bogs. At least, most men don't. Certainly not those who build houses on the shores, nor those who swim and splash on beaches, nor those who paddle canoes in quiet corners or follow the wind in sailboats.

The flood plains of mountain-born rivers, the peaceful retreats of glacier-left marshes and lakes, the forest creeks and ponds, these are the waters of Puget Sound man's home neighborhood.

Spruce Creek, Millersylvania State Park.

Baker River, North Cascades National Park.

Green River Gorge, near Black Diamond.

Kayaking on the Skykomish River.

Dunn Canyon, once an exciting kayak trip, now is drowned by a Tacoma City Light dam which was built over protests of fishermen, white-water clubs, and other conservationists.

Curley Creek. Pacific Power and Light wants to flood this creek and a nearby natural arch.

Fishing the Skykomish River.

Quinault River and the Enchanted Valley trail bridge.

"Lake" Cushman from the Mt. Ellinor trail. The real, the natural Lake Cushman was drowned long ago by a Tacoma City Light dam.

Boyle Lake and Fuller Mountain, on the Weyerhaeuser Company's Snoqualmie Tree Farm.

Salmon leaping falls on the Soleduck River, Olympic National Park.

Flood plain of the Snohomish River.

Steelhead fishermen on the Green River.

Deer Creek and Wheeler Mountain, near Oso.

Takhlakh Lake and Mt. Adams.

Water lilies in Bald Hill Lake.

Lake Lytle, Oregon.

Snoqualmie Falls, a widely-advertised tourist attraction. However, Puget Power turns off the water when peaking power is needed.

Okanogan River, near Omak.

Canoeing on Potholes Reservoir.

Sand-dune islands in Potholes Reservoir, which flooded a lovely dune area, creating a striking pattern of islands. But with the sand source drowned the dunes have lost their sustenance and it's only a matter of wind and time until the islands literally are blown into the water.

Snake River and the entrance to Hells Canyon. Here, for 5 years, Floyd Harvey waged a one-man war against private and public power interests, who were fighting between themselves for the right to flood this canyon, deepest in the United States. Floyd Harvey now has the help of conservation groups all over the nation and maybe the canyon will be saved.

Palouse Falls.

The primeval Baker Lake from the old campground. The lake since has been drowned by a Puget Power reservoir with ghastly shores of mud and stumps.

Skagit River from Sauk Mountain.

Powerboats pulling water-skiers on Lake Sammamish. A pretty picture? Yes. But don't expect to catch any fish, or hear any sounds of wind or songs of birds, or enjoy any moments of quiet contemplation, anywhere in the vicinity.

Evening sailboat races on Lake Washington.

Grand Coulee Dam and Banks Reservoir.

Steamboat Island and Banks Reservoir.

*Two Captains Rock and the reservoir behind John Day Dam on the
Columbia River.*

Indians fishing at Celilo Falls on the Columbia River. This historic spot, where Indians hand-fished for salmon from time immemorial, has since been flooded by The Dalles Dam.

Columbia River, a few miles above Bonneville Dam.

Log rafts on the Columbia River, near White Salmon.

Columbia River port at Longview.

White Salmon River bridge, Columbia River, and Mt. Hood.

Canada geese, near Puget City.

Abandoned salmon cannery at Chinook, near the mouth of the Columbia River.

Columbia River and The Dalles Bridge, with Mt. Hood in distance.

Ship entering the mouth of the Columbia River.

CHAPTER V

INLAND SEA

Strictly speaking, Puget Sound is that specific body of water extending south from Whidbey Island past Seattle and Tacoma and Olympia and curling back north, almost meeting Hood Canal and making the Kitsap Peninsula an island. Commonly, though, the term is used (as I do often in these pages) in an extended if inexact sense to describe the entire system of salt-waterways and bordering lands—Strait of Juan de Fuca, Strait of Georgia, Hood Canal, and the scores of passages, passes, channels, straits, inlets, sounds, ports, harbors, and bays.

A remarkable inland sea it is—in certain respects perhaps unique on Earth—with nearly 2000 miles of waterfront in Washington alone and vastly more northward in Canada along the Inland Passage to Alaska.

A various and diverse sea it is.

From a headland of Whidbey Island, looking out the Strait of Juan de Fuca between the Olympic Peninsula and Vancouver Island, one feels the closeness of the ocean—especially when the sun sinks into a horizon of water or when storm winds blow unobstructed from the Pacific.

Up the Sound, by contrast, where trees crowd the shore, one could mistake inlets for lakes were it not for the rise and fall of tides.

In narrow channels the tidal rush is violent; in shallow bays the water seems stagnant.

The average temperature of Puget Sound varies only several degrees from winter to summer, and on beaches swept by swift currents is always cold; in quiet bays, in summer, when the incoming tide passes over sun-warmed sands, the water becomes tepid, even soupy.

A sea full of islands it is—large ones, and Kitsap Peninsula really the largest of all, small ones, and tiny rocks barely above high tide—islands by the hundred.

Transportation experts have discussed ways and means to build a bridge from Seattle across Puget Sound. The problem is, a bridge in effect destroys an island, and this one would have to land either on Vashon Island or Bainbridge Island, and the inhabitants of both want to remain islanders, insulated by water from mainland Seattle. They argue that the option of the island way of life should be preserved as a distinctive amenity of Puget Sound.

Islands for living and islands for vacation—among them the summits of a drowned mountain range, the San Juan Islands, an archipelago including such tall peaks as Mount Constitution and also little wave-washed rocks set aside as bird sanctuaries, and a maze of passages and coves that probably no one boatman ever has explored completely.

Thousands of weekend and vacation sailors are busy at the exploration—in the San Juans, up and down the Sound, and all the way to Alaska. The inland sea has one of the largest fleets anywhere in the world of small boats—power cruisers, rowboats, sailboats, kayaks, and canoes—and throughout the year the skippers and crews are braving the open reaches, poking into hidden inlets, prowling byways of the water road once traveled by Indian dugouts and later by the "mosquito fleet" of passenger and freight steamers.

The mosquito fleet is now a memory kept alive only by a few excursion boats—but there are still ferries. To be sure, Hood Canal has been bridged and most of the long-haul routes have been eliminated, and on the principal runs obscenely-fast "superferries" have cut trip times in half and to that extent shrunk Puget Sound. However, ferries continue to offer short voyages across the Sound and long ones to Vancouver Island from Port Angeles, Horseshoe Bay, and best of all, through the San Juans from Anacortes, and if the ambitions of engineers can be held in check the ferry rides on the water road will forever add holiday delight to life on the inland sea.

One way to know the water is to navigate the surface by private boat or ferry. Another is to walk the shores—the sandspits and points, deltas and estuaries, salt marshes and mudflats, beaches and bluffs—picnicking or swimming or simply wandering the margin of land and water to see the waves, the shells, the pebbles, the birds, the views of mountains, and the drama of a summer sunset behind the black skyline of the Olympics.

Few west-side Indians lived far from the shores because for them, when the tide was out, the table was spread. Most white invaders also stuck close to the water, partly because travel through virgin forests was difficult, and partly because in hard times a supper of clams was easy and cheap. Even today, few Puget Sounders live more than a half-hour's drive from the tides. The inland sea remains the center, the essence.

Madrona tree overlooking Saratoga Passage from Camano Island State Park.

State park moorage on Jones Island.

Dungeness Spit and the Strait of Juan de Fuca.

Ferryboat in Rich Passage between Bainbridge Island and the Kitsap Peninsula.

Air view of log rafts on Sinclair Inlet, near Bremerton.

Fishing wharf in Salmon Bay, Seattle.

Oyster cannery, South Bend.

At anchor off Sucia Island.

Crew of the ketch Tatoosh.

San Juan Islands.

Snow geese on the Skagit Game Range.

Air view of Puget Sound: in foreground, Hammersley's Inlet; center, Hope Island: left, Squaxin Island; in distance, Danas Passage.

Backwater along the Strait of Juan de Fuca.

Fishing off Lopez Island.

Ferryboat leaving Edmonds. Olympic Mountains on the horizon, with Mt. Washington to the left and The Brothers to the right.

LaConner on Swinomish Channel, with Mt. Baker beyond.

Cormorants at Fort Ward State Park on Rich Passage.

Duckabush Valley and Olympic Mountains. The old barn is gone now. In its place is a tract of nondescript summer homes dotting the field behind the pond.

Puyallup River and the moon rising over Mt. Rainier.

CHAPTER VI

OCEAN WATER

The ocean is the edge of the continent, the horizon that swallows the sun, the margin of a mystery. The ocean is surf and sand and shingles and sea stacks and caves and tidal pools and driftwood and bluffs and dunes. The ocean is peace. And terror. And delight. And reverential awe. The ocean is a state of mind—and soul.

Looking west to the unknown, often I feel spooky, wondering what's out there that might come ashore. A tsunami or typhoon? Some rough beast? Sea and land are at constant war—pity innocent bystanders caught in the middle of a battle! Especially I feel uneasy when our family gang is sleeping under a flimsy tarp a few feet from the surf and the breakers pound closer and closer in the darkness—and what guarantee this night's tide will not rise higher than any in recorded history and engulf our camp and the forests and the continent?

We've walked the beaches in soft summer mist, the sun now and then bursting between gray billows. And we've walked in winter sunshine, watching black squalls roll by out to sea, until one veers and washes us down with a shower of cold rain, followed by blue sky and bright sun. We've walked at night in a full moon, the white foam ghostly. And at night with no moon, no flashlight, feeling the way by foot, straying too far out on the sands and suddenly up to the ankles in sneaky-silent water. And storms! Gale-driven rain in a barrage of stinging bullets, the ocean unseeable except in blinks, violent waves lifting the driftwood mass and hurling it against the thicket of trees bounding the beach, hundreds of tons of logs jumbling and tumbling in a frightening roar.

To walk the Northwest ocean in all its moods, in all seasons, is to learn things about nature and man, life and death, that never can be put in words or even music. You have to be there.

British Columbia, from Vancouver Island north, offers a coastline little changed from Indian days, and as yet known in its entirety to few white men.

Oregon has the finest sand dunes, the longest stretch of picturesque and easily-accessible coast; in the opinion of some ocean-lovers its steep sea meadows on hills high above the breakers are the most glorious single spectacle of the American Pacific.

Washington has sand dunes too, though much smaller, and salt marshes where millions of birds live the year around or during migration, and miles of beaches close to the highway.

But Washington has a special ocean that no longer exists anywhere else in the 48 conterminous states — wilderness ocean. From the Hoh River to LaPush, and from Rialto Beach to Cape Alava, Olympic National Park provides a buffer between civilization and surf.

Begin, say, from the road-end at Ozette Lake. Walk the Park trail through mist-fed, wind-toughened trees, a jungle of head-high salal and slow-moving creeks. Amid the stillness of greenery, pause to listen. What sound is that? Imagination?

Walk a bit more, stop again. Not imagination! Walk faster. Now it can be heard even while hiking, a far-off, constant thunder.

Hastily through a grove of tall firs atop a bluff—and see the ranks of white crests rushing toward the sand, the explosions of spray around stacks, and hear the crash of each breaker, and run down the trail onto the beach.

The wilderness beach. The way it was before Columbus. The way the Indians knew it over thousands of years, ever since they completed the long journey from Asia, a continent far, far beyond that horizon of water.

No more running. Stand and look. Breathe sharp winds scented with salt and seaweed and clams. Walk slowly. Think. Feel.

Here is where all the water comes from, and where it all goes.

The ocean is the beginning—and the end.

The ocean from Second Beach near La Push, Olympic National Park.

Three-ton anchor from the bark Austria, shipwrecked at Cape Alava in an 1887 gale.

Air view of North Point Lighthouse, near Long Beach, Washington.

*Driftwood near Hoh Head,
Olympic National Park.*

*Remains of the Catala, wrecked
near Ocean Shores in 1965.*

Winter storm at Ruby Beach, Olympic National Park.

Surf at Short Sand Beach near Rockaway, Oregon.

Bandon Rocks on the Oregon coast.

Winter storm at Kalaloch Beach, Olympic National Park.

Smelt fishing at Kalaloch Beach, Olympic National Park

Sunset on the Oregon coast at Bandon. Fifteen years ago this was a wilderness beach. Now the shore is lined with private homes, wonderful for the few people who live there.

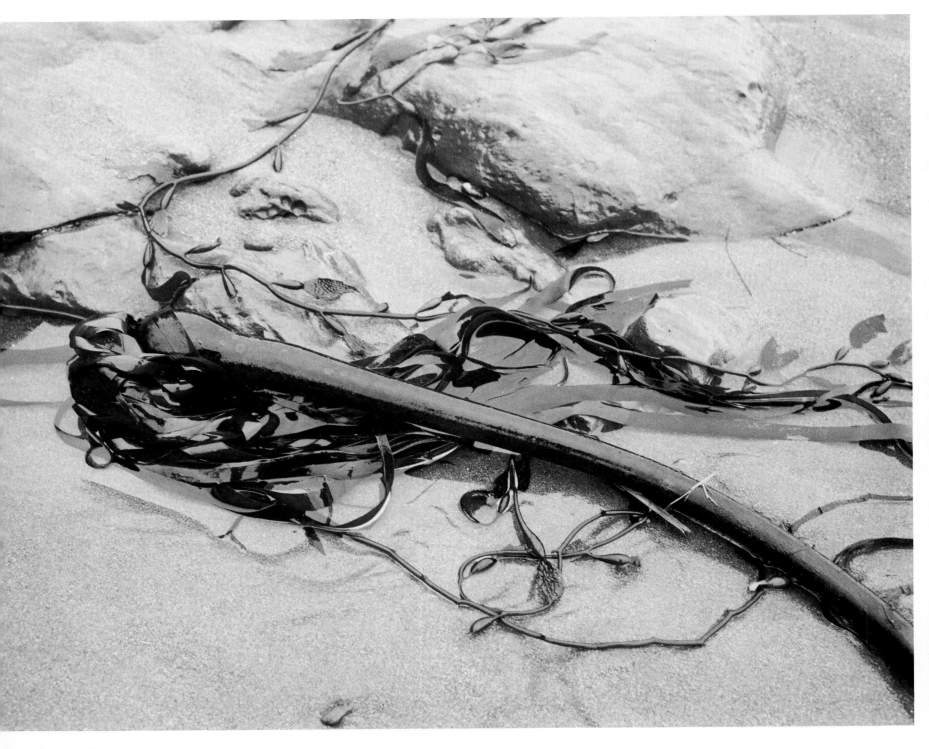

Kelp on Shi-Shi Beach.

Tidal pool at Kalaloch.

La Push, near Second Beach, Olympic National Park.

Rialto Beach and James Island.

Portage Head, north end of Shi-Shi Beach.

Kalaloch Beach.

Sea lions on Oregon coast.

Ecola State Park, Oregon.

Air view, Graveyard of the Giants.

Indian pictographs at Cape Alava.

One of three arches at the south end of La Push beach, but don't look for two of them. The Army Engineers blasted them away for rock ballast to build a harbor jetty.

Pages 152-153. Toleak Point, Olympic National Park.

PROLOGUE

From sky and mountains, rivers and
lakes, to the inland sea and the ocean,
the Northwest is a land of beautiful
water. But will it always be so?
What have we done—and what are we
doing—to our cool and clear, clean
and lovely water?

Snohomish River and an Everett pulp mill.

Industrial waste in the Columbia River at Longview.

CHAPTER VII

HOW WE FOUL OUR WATER

Physiologically speaking, each of us is a perambulating packet of pollution. We enter the world relatively clean—some 90 percent water—but with age get steadily dirtier and as adults are 25 percent pollutants.

Merely by existing, we contaminate. However, widely-dispersed humans living in primitive modes don't bother water more than other animals. The damage is done by too many people, too crowded, too civilized.

How much water does each of us dirty daily by flushing the toilet, washing crockery in a multi-stage electric dishwasher, and taking soapy, perfumed baths to attain the condition next to godliness? (Which is, of course, sexiness.) Then there's watering the lawn we've doused with fertilizer and the flowers we've sprayed with bug-killer and hosing down the driveway we've enriched with gas and oil and grease.

I vividly recall the arid year our family well went dry in May and stayed dry until January. With all water hauled from the city, my wife and I found we could manage on about five gallons a day—including flushing the toilet when absolutely unavoidable, though not counting occasional showers at the homes of friends.

Even during that dry spell, when we treasured every drop of liquid and learned a frugal system of multiple-use, our visible consumption of water was only a fraction of our real consumption.

Consider paper alone. The books (including this one) and newspapers and magazines, the food packages, the handy tissues, the wallpaper, the cardboard, the fiberboard, and on and on. Don't ask who's responsible for those river-poisoning sky-smirching pulp mills. *We* are. You and me.

How many rivers are drowned for hydro power, how many other rivers and bays heated up or dirtied up for thermal power, coal-fired or nuclear, so we can simultaneously illuminate every room in the house and also the yard and street and skyline and clouds above, so we can have a tank of hot water constantly available even when we are asleep or away on vacation, so we can wear out clothing prematurely by incessant washing and drying, so we can brush our teeth and carve the turkey without exercising arm and wrist muscles? And while noting our luxurious waste of electricity, never forget the torrent of aluminum that pours daily from supermarket through house to garbage can; the making of this metal requires such extravagant quantities of power it may be taken as the symbol of the wanton way of American life—unless that honor better belongs to television, which draws enormous amounts of juice and constantly prods the viewer to buy-use-waste-pollute.

How much fouled water is represented by each of the one, two, or three automobiles in the garage or carport? And how much more by the gas and oil required to keep "muscle machines" functioning as sublimers of psychic and sexual frustrations and as prime producers of evil-ized air?

None of us, moving through our routines of living as skinsful of polluted water, each of us personally dirtying 139 gallons of water a day (City of Seattle average), each of us using or misusing hundreds of more gallons a day by purchasing the goods and services of a rich and reckless civilization, can pretend to holiness. Who spilled the oil on Santa Barbara beaches? You did, Mr. and Mrs. American Motorist. And me too. Who is now plotting to destroy the Alaskan tundra? Guilty again. Who is killing the Great Lakes? You are, Mr. Owner of a Detroit iron. (I drive a foreign car and foul un-American waters.)

Every moderately-alert citizen of our nation has heard from teachers and scientists and journalists and government

Roadside along US 101.

Eastern Washington apple orchard. Chemicals applied to nourish trees and kill bugs flush into waterways, with dire effects on aquatic life and wildfowl.

officials that: (1) we are as a species mostly water; (2) for many of our necessary life purposes, only fairly clean water is acceptable; (3) we are currently dirtying more water than natural processes can clean; (4) we are such potent polluters already, and have such a preposterous expansion of the Gross National Product on the drawing boards, that the rivers and lakes we foul today are mere tokens of the oceans we will foul tomorrow; (5) the way things are going, in a future eon the sludge worms will look back upon us as we now look back on the dinosaur.

The problem here in the Northwest is that we still have so much cool, clear water, so much lovely, sparkling water, we find it hard to believe we'll ever be so beastly as our cousins elsewhere. How could we conceivably mess *our* nest so horribly?

Let me count the ways....

Dirty Water in the Sky

See the plume from the copper smelter, the pall from the pulp mill, the miasma from the freeway.

When the rain comes down, "it isn't raining rain, you know, it's raining nitric acid." Plus other chemicals noxious to violets and people. Rain cleans the polluted sky—briefly, afterward, we view the Olympics and Cascades before industrial stacks and infernal combustion machines refill the atmospheric cesspool. But carry an umbrella, don't trust the rain. Even before water falls from the heavens onto earth we've begun to dirty it.

Scientists boring holes in the Blue Glacier of Mount Olympus have found DDT in the ice, carried there by winds blowing off the Pacific Ocean. The DDT in Olympic National Park, "a museum of primitive America," drifts around the world from wheatfields of the Soviet Union, potato patches of Germany, cornfields of Iowa, apple orchards of Yakima, rose gardens of Bellevue.

Testing of nuclear bombs (except by the reckless nations of France and China) is usually underground nowadays, with only "acceptable emissions" to the surface, and these in areas where "it doesn't matter." However, plans are being drawn to site power-producing nuclear infernos adjacent to every city of every civilized nation.

Environmentalists fervently hope nuclear engineers will free us from dependence on river-damming and fossil-fuel burning. But no existing nuclear power plant is perfectly fail-safe or has a perfectly clean stack. There can be such if the price is paid for safety and purification devices, but in their jubilant rush toward civilian respectability the "nukes" would prefer "acceptable emissions" and the consequent deaths — one here, one there, countless thousands in total over the continents and the years, but no worse than smoking cigarettes, which also is legal

Do we dare trust the nukes? Seattle City Light wants to build a nuclear plant on Kiket Island. The proposed design wastes energy in the form of un-used heat. To get rid of (rather than find a way to use) the heat, the intention is to flush it into salt water—the cheapest method under present technology. Does Seattle City Light care that the flushing would raise the temperature of adjacent waterways from an average 50-60°F to 70-80°? Apparently not. These honorable civil servants have acquired land for the installation without studies of the full, long-range effects on the marine ecosystem.

If the public utility is so blithe about heating a bay, must we not wonder how much it knows or cares about the radioactivity the plant would spew into our air?

The sky is a menace to life and health. It's loaded with nitric acid from jet aircraft and lead from automobiles and sulfuric acid from smelters and pulp mills and fluorides from aluminum plants. But don't bother with an umbrella. The radioactive rain will get you in the city and it will get you in the wilderness. There's no way, no where, to escape.

I see a lanky girl bounding in slow motion through a meadow in a mist, trailing a glory of swirling hair. She laughs with the joy of running free, the cold wash of wind-driven water on her cheek. She lifts her arms to embrace the cloud, opens her mouth, takes a deep swallow of sky water, looks terribly sexy, and topples over dead. —A pity. She didn't even have time to finish the cigarette commercial.

Stuck in the mud on Naches Pass. The pioneers' wagon trail, famous in history and legend, is being obliterated by mechanized recreationists.

Dirty Water in the High Hills

Driving east from North Bend a couple autumns ago, we noted the Snoqualmie River was extraordinarily muddy. On a side-trip to the Alpental ski area and real-estate subdivision (to mourn the plundering of a fondly-remembered alpine valley) we saw why. Ski slopes were being "groomed" and tons of soil were washing and sliding into a chocolate-brown Source Creek. Later I read in the papers that fishermen were irate at the total wipe-out of their sport in the Snoqualmie for weeks that fall. Tough luck, Izaak! There's a law against muddying water but it's not enforced.

Really, the state hardly could prosecute private industry for what the state does all the time. Even as Alpental was converting the crystal-rippling Source Creek to a dirty ditch, the State Highway Department was filling and paving a meadow-marsh at the summit of Snoqualmie Pass and mangling the entire South Fork Snoqualmie River to build Interstate 90. And see what bulldozers have done to Ruby Creek and Granite Creek and Early Winters Creek while constructing the North Cross State Highway. And see how Swauk Creek has been maltreated by the new Swauk Pass Highway—unlike the old Blewett Pass Highway, which followed the same valley but allowed the creek decent running room.

The highwaymen and ski-slope groomers and loggers either don't know or don't care how many thousands of years have been required to accumulate the thin mantle of mountain soil they shove so wrecklessly into streams, and they either don't understand or ignore the intricate balance of forces represented by a natural watercourse. Tinker with one segment of a river or creek and the effects extend in a chain reaction upstream and downstream. The consequences of ruthless, mindless bulldozing already done in mountains of the Northwest will continue for decades, generations, or centuries.

And the earthmovers roar on. Slopes are denuded to bare rock, river channels are pushed out of the way of roads, and the waters run muddy after every heavy rain.

Sometimes a river takes revenge. To make space for Interstate 90 in the vicinity of the upper terminal moraine of the ancient Puget Glacier, the Highway Department relocated the Snoqualmie. Came a torrential rain and in few hours the river tore out all four lanes of new concrete. The night is vivid in my memory; I was possibly the last person to drive the disintegrating highway and live. The engineers almost killed me.

Big machines ravage rivers. Smaller machines crummy creeks and mash meadows. It began with World War II jeeps and civilian successors and the formation of oily packs of four-wheel drivers dedicated to advancing the American frontier beyond highways and logging roads into high tundra. The limitations of four wheels stirred the demon inventors, excited by nightmares of an entire nation of Hell's Angels, to perfect the trailbike, and this was so successful they followed with the dune-buggy, the snowmobile, the marsh-buggy, the hovercraft, the "all-terrain vehicle," and now Wall Street is observing with interest the "growth industry of sportsmobiles." Lord, it is time for the thunder.

Sportsmobiles pollute quiet, pollute air. And see the jeep and trailbike ruts in the marshes and soft-soiled flower gardens, across the creeks, around the shores and shallows of alpine lakes. See the oil slicks. In steep meadows, see the gouges of a hill-climbing contest, scars of a single afternoon of wanton fun that will remain after the bike-jockeys are dead and forgotten and unlamented.

The U.S. Forest Service, apostle of "multiple-use," eagerly accepts wheels as the equal of feet and is delighted to list another "use" in its annual reports of service to the nation. But one

Highway construction on the Olympic Peninsula, a typical example of brutality to the soil, the vegetation, and the watercourse.

infamous summer weekend thousands of bike-riders rendez-voused in the Little Naches valley. A lone ranger tried to control the mob. The easy riders offered to hang him to the nearest pine. He shut up and went away, mumbling. Now the entire Forest Service, shaken by this and similar experiences, stews in the rotten mess of "multiple-abuse" and awaits with resignation the only solution, the final thunder.

Before machines, there were animals in the hills. On occasion I've been offended by the indelicacies of bear or deer, and more often by the churning and wallowing of elk, but the wild beasts came first and I can't justly complain. However, I vigorously object to the bands of sheep and herds of cattle prodded by man into Cascade high country. Walk an alpine garden in the wake of these misplaced domestic animals. The flowers are gone, the air reeks, and the water is tainted. One thirsty day of roaming the west flank of Mount Adams I was forced to climb above demolished flowers, even above bouldery moraines, all the way to the snout of the Adams Glacier before finding drink-able water flowing from the ice. "Hoofed locusts," John Muir called sheep. He forgot to mention the stench. Nor did he ever,

as have I, belatedly find himself drinking the sewage from cow pies deposited in meadow creeks of Horseshoe Basin and Cho-paka Mountain.

Horses are likeable and useful creatures and it's not their fault they are big and heavy and therefore stomp marshy creeks into black muck and excrete enormous masses of stinking pollutant. If properly tended, horses in limited numbers can travel virtually any mountain area (that they are physically capable of traveling) without excessively disturbing the terrain or other visitors. Some owners of horses, however, have such crude habits they should be confined to barns for life. I've seen horses staked in the small spring that supplies the only water at Cascade Pass, and horses wading in Image Lake and releasing ballast precisely where I had been, until then, filling my water bucket. Both horses and camping are now banned at Cascade Pass and from the shores of Image Lake, but elsewhere are other streams and lakes which continue to be abused—not by innocent horses, but careless horse-owners.

At this point I wish I could offer as ultimate hero and practicing saint the alpine pedestrian who climbs laboriously to the

Junior members of The Mountaineers cleaning up Copper Lake. Sad to say, many mountain travelers, as well as many cities and counties, look upon lakes as convenient places to dump garbage.

highland on his own two feet and is so respectful of Nature he never, ever dirties the water.

Sad to say, there are too few candidates for sainthood. The backpack is not necessarily the badge of virtue. See rusty water oozing from meadows where somebody, years ago, carefully buried garbage. See alpine lakes with shores and shallows covered by tin cans and aluminum foil and broken glass. See entrails of fish in creeks. See the revolting evidence of a human having emptied his bowels in a watercourse instead of in adjacent woods. And see clean-and-neat campers wash dishes in a stream, loosing food particles and detergent into somebody else's drinking water.

When I began walking Northwest hills a short three decades ago, it was an article of faith and a proud boast that "mountain water is good water." But recreationists have become so numerous in the Cascades and Olympics, and so many are either untaught newcomers or outright slobs, nowadays one must be wary of highland water.

Drowning Rivers and Lakes

A number of dams built in the Northwest in past years for city water, irrigation water, hydroelectric power, and other purposes may be judged economically wise and socially beneficial—at least from the short-run standpoint of the citizens immediately involved. However, some existing dams caused damage that would make them highly controversial were they now to be proposed, and if there's any new dam planned hereabouts that satisfies contemporary environmentalist criteria, I haven't heard of it.

Why, then, are scores of dams being designed and promoted, and why is virtually every free-flowing stream in danger? Because a lot of people earn a living building dams and they are resisting technological unemployment more vigorously, if that is possible, than the generals.

Consider two federal agencies, the Bureau of Reclamation and the Army Corps of Engineers, which long ago completed every useful dam possible under their jurisdiction in the region and since then, to perpetuate bureaucratic empires, have been busy building useless dams. (Not entirely useless—not if you're a Congressman or Senator or County Commissioner basing your reelection campaign on how deep you've dipped your snout in the pork barrel—and not if you're a land speculator or contractor or cement-sand-gravel supplier.)

Consider the power companies—Seattle City Light, Tacoma City Light, PUD's, and private firms—managed by anachronisms who feel genuine physical pain and moral outrage when they hear the sound of running water—unless it's pouring through a turbine.

The engineers and bureaucrats who have devoted their careers to blocking the natural flow of water will never rest so long as a single river, anywhere, runs free—"wasted."

Not to rake up old bitterness, but to suggest the full environmental cost of existing and proposed dams, keeping in mind that pollution of water is only one way to foul it up, let us sample the accomplishments and ambitions of the dam gang.

Irrigation. The retreat of mountain glaciers formed a natural Lake Keechelus, a natural Lake Kachess, and a natural Lake Cle Elum. Farmers found that for minor expense they could raise nature's dams, drown the lakes, and store more water for summer irrigation. Now when the reservoirs are drawn down the shores are a wasteland of mud and stumps. A reservoir is never a "lake," no matter how often the term is misapplied.

There is a scheme to enlarge Bumping Lake, flooding a valley floor heavily used for recreation. There is an irrigation-electricity plot to reservoir-ize Lake Wenatchee, one of the most popular recreation sites in the state, threatening the superb inlet area where the river meanders amid marshes that provide homes and breeding grounds for thousands of birds and beasts. The same plan would dry up the spectacular rapids of Tumwater Canyon and flood a long stretch of the Chiwawa River. Fewer trees. Less wild water. More mud.

Flood Control. The Army Corps of Engineers built the Howard Hanson Dam on the Green River to protect farms from flooding. Industry and homes moved in, taxes went up, and farms went out. And because the plain is now full of buildings and because neither dams nor dikes can control rainwater from nearby hills, flood damage is greater (though not so dramatic) than before the Army arrived.

The Engineers yearn to cap their Green River fiasco with a vastly more ambitious and moronic molestation of the Snoqualmie-Skykomish-Snohomish Rivers. The soldiers have in mind an ultimate system of dams on all the main streams and tributaries, enough to keep a regiment at work well into the next century.

Ross "Lake" at Hozomeen. From February through June, the Seattle City Light reservoir is nowhere in sight from here. Instead, the valley is a vast desolation of mud and stumps, the remains of a magnificent forest. If Seattle has its way and raises Ross Dam, the devastation will be extended 9 more miles north into Canada.

To get the bulldozers rolling, the Corps proposes a foot-in-the-door dam on the Middle Fork Snoqualmie, drowning 10 miles of river. However, since this one dam cannot be justified on the original grounds of flood control, the Army drums are pounding the theme of recreation.

Recreation! On a reservoir that would be drawn down 10 vertical feet in summer, exposing a wide belt of shore mud. In King County, which has 760 lakes and thus no shortage of still-water recreation. And how about the loss of flowing-water recreation and forest recreation for trout fishermen, kayakers and canoeists, deer and grouse hunters, hikers, picnickers, and wildlife watchers?

The Army also says the dam will "not necessarily" mean loss of the Snoqualmie green belt so badly needed to provide relief from solid urbanization. The King County Council agrees, and in supporting the dam vows to zone the flood plain to keep it green. The dairy ranchers declare their firm intention to continue raising cows, and never mind the blandishments of real-estate speculators carrying satchels of cash. Surely we can believe the King County Council, nearly half of whose members are in the real-estate game, and the Snoqualmie farmers, who are so fond of the land they wouldn't care to become millionaires like their Green River brethren.

One must wonder, though, whether there aren't higher-priority calls for the $49,000,000 in public money that would be expended on the Middle Fork dam. Not to mention the further dams on the North Fork Snoqualmie, on branches and tributaries of the Skykomish, and the hundreds of millions of dollars to be dipped from the pork barrel over decades ahead.

For much less money the people of America could purchase development rights to the entire flood plain and thereby prevent the erection of buildings where they don't belong (thus eliminating the possibility of significant flood damage) and keep the area in open-space, green-belt farms. This low-budget proposal would also preserve the wild rivers. However, it would have absolutely no benefits for the Army Engineers and the real-estate vultures.

Hydro-electricity. The historic "River of the West," the Columbia, has been ponded from Bonneville Dam to Canada—except for one final 57-mile stretch between the McNary Dam Reservoir and Priest Rapids Dam. The Army Engineers propose to finish the job with Ben Franklin Dam, which would allow barge travel to Wenatchee and add a few more kilowatts to the Northwest power pool, but is so dubious economically the soldiers have had to extend the pay-out period from the usual 50 years to 100 to get a "do-build" cost-benefit ratio. The losses? The last opportunity in Eastern Washington to feel intimately the impressive power of the mighty river flowing free, the associated fishing, hunting, and camping, and 60 identified archeological sites.

The Corps can and must be beaten on this ludicrous scheme. But northward in Canada, Mica Creek Dam is beyond stopping; the entire Big Bend of the Columbia will be drowned, a tragedy few North Americans are protesting, but one that will be mourned after the deed is done and people of the continent awake to the enormity of their loss.

With most of the Columbia dead or doomed, now comes the turn of the Snake River. A series of four dams has been designed by the Army Engineers to permit barge travel 400 miles up the Snake from the Columbia River to Lewiston, Idaho—and generate electricity too. Ice Harbor Dam was first. Lower Monumental Dam, finished early in 1969, flooded the archeological site of Marmes Man, inhabited continuously for 10,000 years and the oldest proven home of man in North America. The Little Goose Dam reservoir was filled in early 1970. Next on the schedule is Lower Granite Dam, which if allowed to proceed will complete the drowning of the Snake River in Washington and in the opinion of sportsmen will seriously damage, if not destroy, whatever remains of the chinook salmon and steelhead runs on the entire Snake.

The same sort of utilizers who desecrated Glen Canyon on the Colorado River, and sought to flood the Grand Canyon itself, want to drown the wildest and most scenic segment of the Snake—Hells Canyon, described by former Secretary of the Interior Stewart L. Udall as "the deepest gorge on the face of the entire planet." The issue is in doubt; two proposals have been made to block the marauders. One is a 10-year moratorium on dam-building on the Snake between Idaho and Oregon. The other calls for a Hells Canyon-Snake National River to prevent dams permanently on the Snake in Hells Canyon, on the lower 100 miles of the Salmon River, and on the lower reaches of the Grande Ronde and Imnaha Rivers.

There have been big power dams on big rivers, and small power dams on small rivers—and on lakes. A half-century ago, local entrepeneurs decided that Lake Chelan, a 55-mile-long inland fjord that ranks among the grandest spectacles of America, should be put to work. They built a cheap little dam and raised the lake level 20 feet to gain a dab of kilowatts and profits to shareholders. In the process they drowned alluvial fans up and down the lake—lands that would be priceless today for recreation—and flooded marshes and meanders of the Stehekin River.

Puget Power, a private utility which periodically turns off the widely-advertised tourist attraction of Snoqualmie Falls, also has drowned with a fluctuating reservoir the primeval Baker Lake at the feet of Mount Baker and Mount Shuksan.

Tacoma City Light, having first built Alder Dam on the Nisqually River and decorated the standard approach to Mount Rainier with the mud and stumps of Alder Lake, bludgeoned fierce resistance by sportsmen and other conservationists and flooded the unique canyons of the Cowlitz River with Mayfield Dam and Mossyrock Dam.

The Cowlitz PUD drowned the old Packwood Lake, entryway to the Goat Rocks Wilderness Area, for a dribble of electricity. The engineers were inept, the reservoir fluctuates out of control, rising to kill trees around the shore, then dropping, leaving snags.

Seattle City Light staked out the Skagit River, largest of Western Washington streams, some 50 years ago. In an era when free rivers were plentiful and visitors to the North Cascades few, the utility went about its business unopposed, building Diablo Dam and then Ross Dam, the latter flooding 24 miles of canyons and forests. The resulting "lakes" are beautiful when full—though not so beautiful to those who knew the waterfalls and gorges and trees and marshes and wildlife habitats lost under the reservoirs.

Now, in an era when free rivers are increasingly scarce, Seattle City Light proposes to complete the 50-year-old scheme by raising Ross Dam 122½ feet, drowning 9 more miles of the Skagit in Canada and 6 miles of Big Beaver Creek and other miles of Little Beaver Creek, Lightning Creek, Devils Creek, and Ruby Creek in the Ross Lake National Recreation Area.

By juggling figures from month to month and one public hearing to the next to meet preservationist objections, Seattle City Light is able to justify to itself the economic practicality of the High Ross Dam. Even so, the utility admits the increment of power would serve increased consumer demands for only 3 years, after which other sources must be developed anyway. And meanwhile the Sales Department is spending money like it's going out of style in an attempt to prod consumers to use more juice.

What would be lost by the building of High Ross? In British Columbia, the best fly-fishing waters left in the Northwest, and most of the only large expanse of valley-bottom recreation lands within close reach of Vancouver—and for this the Canadian people would receive the annual rent of $5.50 (!) for each acre drowned. In the Big Beaver valley, the last large stand of river-terrace western red cedar in the United States, many of the trees more than 1000 years old—and with the cedars, a wildland of marshes and beaver ponds, a rich community of plant and animal life. In the upper Skagit, Big Beaver, and elsewhere, the spawning grounds which sustain the fish population of Ross Lake. And more.

No wild river, no natural lake, is safe from the engineers and bureaucrats, allied with land speculators and politicians, who find job security and professional satisfaction and personal profit in messing up the water. The dam gangsters will continue their depredations until they are all arrested and rehabilitated and given honest jobs.

Gold-mining dredge at Liberty, ruining a river valley to extract a few particles of a "precious metal." The venture is just barely profitable to the miners, and with any value at all placed on the lost resource of a natural watercourse is obviously uneconomic.

Man-Handling Rivers Still Allowed to Run

Do engineers and entrepeneurs ever gaze in awe over a valley, marvel at the intricacy and beauty of the hydraulic system, and reflect how the river made the valley and under a divine scheme has a prior right of occupancy? Do they ever design roads and structures in humble obedience to the commandment, "thou shalt first and above all let the river be?" Certainly not. Except when it can be converted to a commodity—by a dam, say—they treat running water as a nuisance.

Examine any mountain highway and see how the river is distorted and filthied whenever movement of machines can thereby be expedited. Respecting and honoring the river would cost too much.

Timber Industry. Federal authorities recently declared that "logging is one of the most serious sources of water pollution in the Pacific Northwest." A scientist has found that logging along a mountain stream can cause water temperatures to increase as much as 28°F, with serious damage to aquatic life.

Many a time have I walked beside a sparkling stream flowing through shadowed forest—and returned later to find the sun scorching stumps, steel cables, gasoline drums, and raw banks of eroded soil. Gone, all gone, the mossy banks by cool pools, green walls lining an avenue of wild water. It's too expensive, says the timber industry and the Forest Service, to leave a belt of undisturbed greenery along the stream. It's cheap and easy to rape the river and corrupt the creek.

Mining Industry. Drive Swauk Pass Highway and see how gold dredges have digested the valley floor, extracted minute particles of metal, and excreted heaps of sterile gravel. Dredging continues near Liberty. Visit the old mining town of Holden and see the moonscape of poisonous tailings, a blot on the valley visible from miles away. The mine operated for only 20-odd years, but now, a decade after the shut-down, Railroad Creek carries vile chemicals into Lake Chelan and will continue to kill

Logging operation in the Cascade Range. The thin layer of mountain soil, accumulated over thousands of years, often is subject to severe erosion after the bulldozers and trucks have chopped up the terrain. Soil is the basic land resource, and its loss endangers the future of the forest industry. And meanwhile, the soil washed into creeks damages or destroys aquatic life, including fish. And removal of the tree cover raises the water temperature, with further serious consequences to the chain of life.

vegetation and fish for generations, perhaps centuries. Mines at least as large are contemplated on the Suiattle River and the Middle Fork Snoqualmie and elsewhere in the Cascades, some by companies which recognize the burden of proof is upon them that mines and rivers can be good neighbors, but some by companies convinced the best of all possible centuries, the 19th, will never end.

Flood Control! A flood plain is, by definition, part of the river. People must adjust their activities on a flood plain to the needs of the river, and not the reverse. Tell it to the Army Engineers.

The lessons of the Green River demand endless repetition. Besides building a dam the Engineers have diked and riprapped the lower channel to keep the river in its bed. But nature does not intend a river to remain within low-water banks. Nature envisions regular floods, during which the entire flood plain is the river bed.

The Green River, confined unnaturally, is silting up. Some tributaries must be pumped into the elevated bed. Rainwater can't climb over the dikes and thus stands on the "protected" plain. Many more millions in public funds must be spent to dry up the plain and subsidize the people who build where they don't belong. And someday a hell-roaring flood will burst the dikes and devastate the tract houses and industrial plants; the Army's maximum claim is to limit the occurrence of such catastrophes to once or twice a century. Better by far had the valley continued in farms regularly enriched by flood-deposited soil, farms that fed the people of the city and gave green relief from the gray monotony of urbanization.

Once the Sammamish River was a quiet slough winding amid tangles of trees and water plants, the home of animals and birds, a close-to-city wildland for lazy boat-drifting, listening to the songs, watching for the splash of beaver, otter, muskrat. Now

166

and then the water overflowed pastures. The cows didn't mind; the real-estate sharks did. So the Army Engineers tossed another morsel in the pork barrel, the local congressman and county commissioners dipped their snouts to gobble it up, and the Corps straightened and dredged the channel, riprapped the banks, and today the one-time wildlife wonderland of the Sammamish is a drainage ditch.

Navigation. As mentioned earlier, the Army Engineers are spending multimillions of public funds damming and dredging to permit barge traffic to Wenatchee and Lewiston; the Army is inordinately fond of barges and the dream of every inland hamlet is to become a barge port. The ineffable Engineers also proposed to make the town of Concrete a port for ocean-going ships by dredging the Skagit River. Two problems arose. First, nobody could figure why a ship would ever want to go to Concrete. Second, sportsmen instantaneously howled in unanimous outrage. The Corps therefore put the plan in the "cool-it" file to await a more propitious moment.

Garbage. Float down or drive along any lowland stream and

see how farmers, home-owners, and industry use the water as a sewer and the banks as a junkyard. Pass the outfalls of manufacturing plants and note hideous potions issuing forth—despite laws (slowly, very slowly, being enforced) against pollution. See wrecked cars, heaps of rusty cans, worn-out stoves and refrigerators and washing machines, rotten boats, and a hundred other varieties of trash.

One can love a river and still abuse it. In years past, when streams suffered minor pollution until they entered the zone of intensive farming and industry, the water remained relatively pure all the way from the mountains. But note the black slime on rocks of the South Fork Snoqualmie River, colonies of algae growing on nutrients spewed from the "village" at Snoqualmie Pass. Nowadays, with ski resorts in the snow country, crowded public campgrounds in the high valleys, and vacation-home subdivisions filling the low valleys, and swarms of fishermen and picnickers and hunters and boaters everywhere, the rule is, don't drink the water.

The Death of Lowland Creeks

Items from the Seattle newpapers of 1969 and early 1970:

An apartment house invades the channel of Thornton Creek. And its headwater pond is about to be paved to make a parking lot that will pour gas and oil in the creek and downward to Lake Washington.

The central ravine of West Seattle's Puget Park is filled with chemical wastes from a cement plant—until the City Council belatedly calls a halt.

Boise Creek is poisoned with heated water and bark sugars from a sawmill; the water runs dark and slimy and dead.

A pickle company pours vinegar and spices (and pickles) into Newaukum Creek.

A service station leaks gasoline into Kelsey Creek and kills the fish.

An aircraft company kills more fish in Boeing Creek with a discharge of chromium compounds.

A sewer district bulldozes Juanita Creek, covering fish-spawning beds with silt.

A subdivider proposes to drain the effluent from hundreds of tract houses into a sewage lagoon (cesspool) beside Bear Creek.

The ravine of Kiwanis Memorial Preserve, a Seattle park, is used for dumping garbage and debris, partly illegally, partly with a permit from the Seattle Engineering Department.

Hunters in Eastern Washington report waterways littered with wildfowl killed by fertilizer and/or pesticide draining from irrigated farms.

A section of Coal Creek is proposed to be filled with garbage and thus converted into flat, valuable real estate—which would ooze noxious liquid into Coal Creek Regional Park and Lake Washington.

An enormous gravel pit is proposed next to Soos Creek, threatening the Soos Hatchery, a principal source of the trout used to stock lowland streams.

A supermarket dumps waste oil into Mill Creek, and a fuel company spills more in Chambers Creek.

Quilceda Creek is fouled by a construction firm, and Jordan and Issaquah Creeks by a gravel pit, and Lackamas Creek by an egg ranch.

All these are notes of what is happening in the Seattle area. Follow the Vancouver, Portland, and Spokane newspapers; the story is the same. And elsewhere across the nation.

For every creek whose actual or impending death makes the news, a score of others die unreported in the environmental obituaries. Suburban and rural gullies are convenient for night-time dump-and-run garbage disposal. And when surrounding land is covered by houses, a speculator arrives to fill the hole in the ground (become a "public nuisance" anyway) and make more flat land for more houses. At the best, if homeowners or park departments don't destroy a gulch, they "improve" it by clearing native vegetation, landscaping natural slopes to a more pleasing design, and planting exotic flowers and shrubs with a higher social status than skunk cabbage and devils club and nettles and salmonberries.

So it goes. What passes for urban planning is done mostly by real-estate men who dream of Kansas plains and by landscape architects and recreation experts who love pansy patches, lawns, picnic tables, swings, teeter-totters, and an artistic arrangement of trash cans and comfort stations.

Yet give any bunch of kids a choice between an expertly-planned, fully-equipped playground and a plain old wild creek. In an honest ballot the creek will always win. The ravines are hideaways from the adult world, places to build secret camps. Creeks are for wading, for watching and even catching fish, for following tracks of skunks and raccoons, for listening to bird-songs. Creeks are for studying the patient way the running water

Ski resorts at Snoqualmie Pass provide a wonderful opportunity for mass recreation, but are a painful sight to those who fondly recall the pass as it was in the 1930s.

Swamp zoned for commercial development.

erodes banks, builds sandbars grain by grain, steadily digs and fills to establish an even grade. A creek is a living thing. Kids know it. They can spend endless happy hours simply messing around with their friend, the water.

Kids aren't the only ones. Here and there are homes fitted into the landscape by a partnership of nature-sensitive architects and builders and homeowners to allow entire families to live with and enjoy the water, and parks designed to preserve the natural flow, the natural tangle of greenery, and the natural population of fish, birds, and animals. But the examples are few and scattered.

Urbanizing man treats water as a nuisance, shoves it around to suit his constructions and tries to ignore it. However, between 3 and 5 feet of sky water are dumped on Puget Sound lowlands each year, mostly in winter months. That much water won't be ignored.

On lands covered by forest, a relatively small percentage of the rain runs off immediately, the rest retained by plants or slowly filtered through the soil for delayed release. In a typical "pioneer" suburb, the instant run-off is double or triple that of a forest. As houses crowd in wall to wall, as yards are landscaped with driveways, patios, sidewalks, and formal gardens, nearly all the water rushes away as soon as it falls.

What happens? A honeymoon couple buys a dream house in dry summer—and one wet winter morning awakes in the middle of a lake. Long-time residents of a wooded hillside awake the same morning to find a formerly-sparkling little creek now a muddy torrent tearing at the foundations of their house. The construction of Lake Hills on the heights west of Lake Sammamish has been a disaster to people on the slope below. Similar sad stories are told throughout the Puget Sound country.

To be sure, catch basins and drain pipes and storm sewers can be built, the nuisance water can be held back, put underground, out of sight and mind. Of course, the enormous cost must be paid by the victimized public, not by the quick-footed, fast-dodging subdividers.

Wouldn't it be wiser and cheaper to devote every remaining free-flowing creek and every remaining wild ravine to providing sky water a natural path toward the sea? If you have any doubts on what stand to take on laws that would protect lowland watercourses—not merely the actual channels but also large belts of adjacent woods to hold back and filter the water—don't seek counsel from real-estate experts. Ask your kids.

The Death of Lowland Lakes

Lake Washington was turning brown in summer and beginning to stink. A zoology professor warned that little time was left before the final foul and nasty death. Fat-cat movers-and-shakers, always before complacent about degrading Puget Sound environment in the name of progress and profit, suddenly realized they themselves—not the peasants—would soon be living on the shores of a cesspool. Millions of dollars of public money were spent to divert raw and treated sewage and—hurrah!—Lake Washington was saved from disgrace.

Thus the saga of the new governmental agency known by its acronymn, METRO, as it really was.

Never mentioned in the orgies of civic back-slapping, though, is that man's METRO role is only half the story. The other half is nature's role, as played by the Cedar River, which brings from the mountains into Lake Washington a steady flow of water which is relatively very clean—forest water, flushing water. METRO gets all the credit, but alone couldn't have done the job.

Green Lake, a scenic and recreational gem in the heart of north Seattle, was murking-up earlier each summer, worse each summer. Dredging was tried, chemicals were applied, and nothing reduced the menace of the "Green Lake crud" afflicting swimmers unwary enough to immerse themselves in the algae soup—not until mountain water, forest water from the Cedar River was piped in. Now Green Lake has been saved, and hurrah again.

What about the hundreds of other lakes in Puget Sound lowlands? Can they be saved? How?

Lowland creeks and lowland lakes are dying together. City and suburb leave no forest land to store and filter the water; rain from streets and yards digs raw gullies, rushes downward thick with mud. There are laws against muddying water, but the laws are not enforced: a creek from Lake Hills has thrust a new delta 180 feet into Lake Sammamish.

The dying creeks carry worse than gravel and mud. Lowland lakes once were fed by clear streams and springs from the

Southcenter, an assemblage of supermarkets and shops covering fertile soil of the Green River valley, which once supplied the people of Seattle with fresh, delicious vegetables. Also, the publisher of this book once hunted wildfowl here—as did countless other sportsmen of his generation. The Army Engineers and the real-estate crowd have changed all that forever.

An apartment house intrudes into Puget Sound, making a marvelous place for a few people to live but blocking the beach walk formerly enjoyed by thousands.

woods; now, surrounded by urbanization, they receive the rinsings of roofs, yards, carports, streets, and highways, a villainous brew of oil and gas and fertilizer and pesticide—the latter particularly significant because 40 percent of the pesticide used in America is applied in urban settings. All Puget Sound lakes have been moving steadily since the Ice Age through a natural sequence which leads ultimately to peat bogs. But man, by enormously increasing the nutrient supply with drippings from automobiles, fertilizer from lawns, overflow from septic tanks and sewer lines, plus goodies added by business and industry, is speeding the process. Algae thrive on the richness of nutrients, the algae population explodes, followed by an explosion in the population of organisms which decompose the algae and in doing so consume oxygen and release carbon dioxide. Fish cannot live in the oxygen-deficient water. The lake stinks from decomposing algae. Property values drop, recreation values vanish.

Lake Sammamish, whose only water supply is lowland creeks being invaded by suburbs, is in danger. The clarity of the lake improved in the summer of 1969, when Issaquah sewage was intercepted by METRO, but subdivision of the drainage basin goes on. Unlike Lake Washington, here METRO does not have the partnership of a Cedar River; there is no inexpensive way to supply mountain water, flushing water. And if Lake Sammamish

dies, will we after all have saved Lake Washington, into which the algae-brown waters will flow?

And if so large a lake as Sammamish is in peril, what of smaller lakes?

Pollution is one way to kill a lake. Another is bulldozing and subdividing the watershed, upsetting the balance between inflow and outflow. Where once the shoreline was relatively stable, now the level may rise abruptly after a storm and flood homes, then drop sharply in dry spells and expose a belt of muck. From many urbanizing areas come reports of lakes newly erratic, and agonized intimations that pollution aside, lakeside real estate is a risky investment.

If we don't wish to take the strenuous measures required to save Sammamish and other lakes, there's an easy solution—fill them up. And sure enough, the developers are working at it. Lake Union has been reduced to a fragment of the original extent and may yet dwindle to a narrow ditch walled by office buildings and apartments. Lake Washington shrank a half-century ago when the Army Engineers lowered the level to build the ship canal to Puget Sound. Large expanses of lake bottom became dry land covered by homes and businesses. New marshes were created, as lovely in their way as the bays they replaced, but all except three of these have since been filled for industrial

Portage Bay on Lake Union. The village of Seattle expanded outward from the shores of Elliott Bay and grew into a city with this lake as a jewel in its very heart. But for 80-odd years the people have allowed exploiters to chip away at the gem. Not much is left, and not much time to save the still-splendid remnant.

sites, apartment buildings, and a University of Washington parking lot. Now open water is being filled for more construction, and the encroachment will continue until the people decide whether they really want a Lake Washington.

Lake Chelan also has been assaulted by a mob of land-makers. However, when a new peninsula was plotted by a trailer-park promoter, the State Supreme Court stopped him cold by declaring a public right to use navigable waters *even when they cover private land*—as on Chelan, where such land was flooded when the lake was raised—and as on saltwaterways, where privately-owned beaches are under water at high tide.

Rejoicing is premature. The 1969 court decision probably does not apply to areas where the Army Engineers have established "harbor lines" which give a quasi-land status to navigable waters—including Lake Washington and many Puget Sound bays. And the decision is being appealed and in any event can be overturned by a simple act of the 1971 Washington Legislature.

At this writing some 75 applications for permits to fill on Lake Washington and Puget Sound are temporarily blocked by the court ruling—as interpreted by the Governor. But the Army Engineers have not indicated they will go along with the Governor, and even if they do, it is in appeals beyond the State Supreme Court, and in hot-and-heavy lobbying at the 1971 session of the Legislature that the issue will be settled between water-lovers and land-makers.

There is another way to kill a lake—by misappropriation.

I remember a winter afternoon of light breezes when two of us sailed a cabin sloop from Portage Bay under the Montlake Bridge to Union Bay and out on Lake Washington—and were there becalmed. Sails hung limp, the auxiliary engine was on the fritz, and we had just one miserable paddle. Hours passed. Night fell. Home port was distant. All around—mysteriously far away—were city lights. All around—oddly muted—was the roar of metropolis. How quiet was the winter night. How dark and deep the water. How splendidly lonesome.

I also remember a Fourth-of-July picnic on Lake Sammamish, sitting on a dock amid the the razz-ma-tazz of water-skiers and drag-racers, recalling the fireworks of my non-safe-and-sane childhood and pondering the design of a simple, inexpensive, recreational torpedo.

We submit too tamely to the tyranny of noise sports. Some water should be forbidden absolutely to any activity louder than wading, swimming, paddling, sailing—places to hear wind ripple the water, waves splash, fish rise to gulp a bug, birds call, children laugh.

A more brutal misappropriation of lakes is to purposes for which the presence of water is irrelevant. Lake Washington has not in truth been saved so long as garbage is dumped near the north end and The Boeing Company blocks the south end, so long as Sand Point is devoted to airplanes, so long as the marshes of Mercer Slough and Yarrow Bay Slough are threatened by filling and subdivision, so long as apartments and railroads and industries and parking lots and more and more bridges either invade the waters or wall them off from public enjoyment.

Nor let us forget Lake Union. Along about 1940, an old man described to me how lovely the lake was when he was a youth and Seattle was a village. He grieved the ruined beauties, he denounced the builders of the city as greedy and corrupt boomers, he railed against public neglect over the preceding 60 years. I hope the old man was lucky enough to die without suffering the outrages of the last 30 years. At the same rate, another 30 years will finish Lake Union.

Nor let us overlook any of our other lakes, all being slowly but surely murdered. Nor let us ignore the impending deaths of any of our remaining marshes, peat bogs, and winter-only ponds being filled with garbage, eliminating bird-and-people refuges to make room for shopping centers and subdivisions and city, city, city.

The Perils of Puget Sound

A few years ago there were saltwater beaches to use and to waste and to spare. Not anymore. Beaches are pure gold and the rush is on. Some items from the Seattle newspapers of 1969 and early 1970:

The State Department of Natural Resources (DNR) has announced abandonment of its long-time and inexcusable policy of selling tidelands to any bidder at any price offered—but still will sell when the dollars are piled high enough, and still eagerly peddles 55-year leases. Most of our beaches already have been acquired by private owners and the squandering of our birthright continues.

Boise-Cascade Properties proposes a massive residential and marina development of Anderson Cove on Hood Canal. The developer needs state-owned tidelands to complete the project. As of this writing, the DNR is considering.

Landfills for industry or residential and recreational subdivision are proposed on Birch Bay, Hunter Bay, Fidalgo Bay, Padilla Bay, Port Townsend Bay, Port Gamble, Bremerton, Hoodsport, and Tacoma Narrows.

Marinas, landings, piers, moorages, boat basins, or the like are proposed for Quartermaster Harbor, Day Island Lagoon, Gig Harbor, Steamboat Island, Squaxin Passage, Annas Bay, Seabeck, Miller Bay, Mats Mats Lagoon, Friday Harbor, and Buck Bay—many of these in shallow or narrow waters which would be radically altered in character by concentrated use.

Burlington-Northern Railroad plans to move railroad tracks 200 feet into the Sound on a mile-long stretch north of Carkeek Park, destroying the finest and most popular beach remaining in Seattle; ultimately the railroad would similarly relocate tracks all the way to Mukilteo.

The Ports of Olympia and Tacoma want to build a super-port on the Nisqually Flats, obliterating one of only two large, undisturbed river estuaries left in Puget Sound country and an irreplaceable wildlife range.

An aluminum company attempted to take over Guemes Island, an oil company tried to preempt Port Susan Bay—both were driven off by irate citizens, and bully for them.

But Seattle City Light and a PUD are planning nuclear power plants on Kiket Island and Samish Island, and the thermal pollution alone would raise havoc with the ecosystem.

The State Parks Commission sought to purchase Miller Bay Spit, a prime example of a delicate sandspit and lagoon where man should visit, not live. Subdividers got there first.

So much for recent Seattle newspaper headlines. For the full story, read the real-estate pages, which detail the steady, uncontested subdivision of once-lonesome shores, miles and miles every year. An insight into the developer mentality was given recently by a lumbering firm dating back to pioneer days, advertising a certain tract of beach as offered for sale "by the original owner." (How do you like that, Chief Leschi? The pioneers hanged you 120 years ago for objecting to the theft of your lands and now their heirs say you and your people never existed.)

A cooling-and-settling pond for pulp-mill waste. From here the pol-lutants drain into the bay. No clams, and darn few fish.

Portrait of an exploiter who wants a road built along the last remaining wilderness ocean beach in the 48 conterminous states.

Certainly beaches are to be used, and with some 2000 miles of shoreland on the inland sea of Washington, there is plenty of room for industry, marinas, private residences, public parks, and wildlife refuges. The problem is that for each use there are appropriate places and inappropriate places, and presently the decision is made by profit-seeking entrepeneurs and tunnel-vision bureaucrats—harassed, to be sure, by militant citizens. A Seacoast Management Bill was introduced into the 1970 Washington Legislature, was converted by the DNR into a "Seacoast Give-away Bill," and was therefore defeated by environmentalists. The 1971 Legislature will try again to devise a law enabling a wise long-range plan to accommodate every proper use of the shores. Until then, only the tenuous Lake Chelan decision by the State Supreme Court, policies of the Governor, and citizen vigilance are protecting Puget Sound from developers, DNR, and Army Engineers.

We alter the shore environment by filling tidelands (eliminating clams and oysters), filling salt marshes (eliminating birds), building jetties and seawalls (upsetting marine currents and thus changing the shore contours), and crowding bays and sandspits with homes, marinas, industries. And also we foul the water.

More than 90 percent of the sewage from the Puget Sound basin goes into salt water, and less than 10 percent receives any purifying treatment. Sewage pours from towns and cities, from beach homes, from recreational boaters, from ships, from state-owned ferryboats (flush the toilet and personally pollute). Most of the sewage is raw and reeking, but even when treated, as by METRO, the outflow carries an enormous nutrient supply, potentially threatening a profound disturbance to the marine ecosystem.

Far and away the worst offender is the pulp industry—so much so that Port Angeles, with three mills, produces one-fifth of the waste discharged into the inland sea, more than Seattle and Tacoma together. Pulp liquor poisons the waters of the bays, killing fish, clams, and oysters. A black sludge of wood fibers and chemicals coats the bottoms of the bays; nothing, not even worms or algae, can live in the hellish mess. Mercury wasted by mills is absorbed by fish and shellfish and ultimately by innocent sportsmen. At long last the state is requiring the mills to mend their obnoxious ways, and most firms are cooperating—though even when in full compliance with existing regulations, perhaps by 1976, they will be allowed to dump 20 percent of their waste liquor in the bays, and while legally clean will remain filthy. One company is fighting fiercely to maintain accustomed rights and is so bold as to argue that pulp liquor may be good for fish. At the present pace, pulp mills might become tolerable neighbors by the middle of the 21st century, if by then anyone remains on Earth to be neighbors.

The vegetable-processing industry is the second-worst polluter, and though a very distant second behind the horrendous filthiness of pulpers, has a number of rivers and creeks on its conscience—plus a bay fouled by a brewer.

Then there is dredging for yacht basins and industry, stirring up silt that kills shellfish. And alumina ore ships which anchor in Puget Sound after discharging cargo at the smelters and sweep the debris overboard.

And garbage. Go beachcombing anywhere—amid the milk cartons, the ketchup bottles, the soggy cardboard, the grapefruit rinds, the eternal plastic in a thousand shapes. Garbage from ships. Garbage from recreational boaters. Garbage from homes. ("Low tide—time to carry out the trash.") Garbage from picnickers and campers.

Yet to come, thermal pollution from nuclear power plants, with a dollop of radioactivity for good measure.

And oil. Today the "unavoidable" drippings into Puget Sound from the Anacortes-Ferndale oil-refinery complex and other commercial operations, plus illegal bilge-pumping by visiting ships, total hundreds of tons a year. Recreationists' outboard motors, so inefficiently designed that up to half their fuel is wasted rather than consumed, annually spill an estimated 670,000 gallons of hydrocarbons into Puget Sound. Today there are occasional, scattered oil slicks on the waters and beaches. We'll forget these quickly enough if and when Puget Sound becomes the terminal and refinery center for super-tankers carrying Alaska oil. The 1970 Legislature passed a very tough law against oil spillage, with no limit on the liability of firms responsible, but no amount of money could compensate for the catastrophic aftermath of a super-tanker piling onto a rock. Biologists declare that if Alaska oil passes through the Sound, destruction of the marine ecosystem is a statistical certainty. The only question is when.

And now the oil companies are applying for leases to drill wells on Puget Sound; the DNR is considering. Already British Columbia has granted such leases for the Strait of Georgia.

This inland sea of ours is essentially a closed system, a "lake." Tides move up the beaches and down, through channels and back again, but there is little mixing with the Pacific Ocean. Because there is so much water, so far only a few bays and inlets and coves are actually lethal to fish and clams and people. But there is not so much water we cannot foul it all ultimately. Hood Canal, the southern reaches of the Sound, and certain other shallow bays are particularly vulnerable and can tolerate little—if any—more development than currently exists. And it is within the eventual capacity of our megalopolis-under-construction to kill the entire inland sea.

How do we save the Sound? Remember the example of Lake Washington, where METRO is eliminating the sewage (raw and treated both) and the Cedar River is supplying the pure flushing water. For the next step, a super-METRO must eliminate sewage (treated as well as raw) from the Sound; super-METRO must also keep the rivers pure, providing a steady, clean flow of flushing water from mountains and forests. What name shall we give this super-METRO? None other than the State-of-Washington-and-the-Province-of-British-Columbia. No smaller unit will do.

And even this will be only a start. To save the Sound the ocean must be saved, a task for a super-super-METRO, otherwise known as the United Nations.

In conclusion, hear a plea for seals, octopuses, seagulls, killer whales, and other fish, mammals, and birds. I've no quarrel with legitimate bird-hunters who observe the legal seasons and bag limits and confine their sport to game species. But the pages of this book would ignite if I spelled out the proper punishment for the boatman or beachwalker who carries a rifle or pistol to bang away at gulls and seals and anything else that moves and can't shoot back—and for the aquarium thugs who tour the Sound herding killer whales into nets.

And one day at Rosario Beach I watched SCUBA divers disappear under the surface of the bay and reappear with an octopus in tow. They photographed the trophy in various poses, then threw it back in the water, dead, and went home content. Some groups of divers hold regular competitions, the prize going to the entrant who brings in the most booty—that is, the heaviest weight of now-dead creatures, edible or not. In the few years since the sport became popular, many favorite diving haunts formerly teeming with undersea life have become ecological deserts. Except for a scattering of biology professors, nobody cares enough to object.

The Ultimate Challenge: Fouling the Pacific Ocean

Not long ago a newspaper quoted a big-mouth, idiot-drooling motel owner at Long Beach as saying, "We know its attraction. It is the longest drivable beach in the world and we intend to keep it that way."

Therefore I don't go to Long Beach, or any other section of the coast tricked out to appeal to yahoos who drive automobiles and motorcycles and dune buggies along the sand, rioting among the breakers, tearing up dunes, wrecking the mood for quiet walkers, terrorizing kids building castles, leaving behind a trail of gas and oil and beer cans. One might argue the best plan is to have a Long Beach and an Ocean Shores where slobs may crowd together in their noise and filth, leaving the rest of the coast to those who approach the ocean as a temple.

But the real-estate sharks are hungry and shore developments are proliferating. And though the public has a legal right to use all beaches (except on Indian reservations) up to the high-tide line, subdivisions are violating the sand dunes and wind-shaped clumps of trees which are essential to the total beach experience —and ecology.

Olympic National Park preserves the shore in a natural condition from Kalaloch to the Hoh River, from the Hoh to LaPush, from Rialto Beach to Cape Alava, and from the north border of the Ozette Indian Reservation to the Ozette River. Except for villages on Indian reservations at Hoh and LaPush, the entire coast from Ruby Beach to the Ozette River is wilderness.

There is other *de facto* wilderness on the Ozette Reservation and northward from the Ozette River to Point of Arches and Shi-Shi Beach, but here there is also the menace of subdivision. The thought is intolerable. Washington has the last long stretch of wilderness beach in the conterminous 48 states; every foot still wild should be kept wild. Elsewhere are plenty of highway-side beaches, hucksterized beaches.

More bad news: Olympic National Park extends only down to high tide; the actual surf-swept beach is state land, and though Oregon has banned automobiles and other machines from ocean beaches, Washington even allows airplanes to land, as happens at points right in the middle of the Wilderness Strip. And the State Department of Natural Resources avidly peddles long-term leases for beach-sand mining and oil-well drilling.

Guns. Fishermen shoot seals because they eat a few fish. Sea otters, reintroduced after being wiped out decades ago, are again being slaughtered.

Garbage. At places, almost as bad as on Puget Sound. Garbage from ships at sea, garbage from local residents, garbage from fishermen and clamdiggers and campers.

The Quinault Indians have had enough. Fed up with abandoned junk cars, tons of litter dropped by vacationers, poaching of shellfish and wanton killing of wildlife, the tribe posted its beaches off-limits to whites. Only with the understanding that Quinaults may police their lands, thus preventing visitors from sabotaging traditional tribal conservation policy, has the public again been made welcome—on a trial basis. One might wish all the beaches in the hands of subdividers and the DNR were under Quinault control.

Oil. Many a time on family hikes we've come upon a feebly-fluttering sea bird soaked with sludge, unable to swim or fly. My kids build convalescent shelters of driftwood and offer morsels from our lunch, but of course the death was certain before we arrived.

From where comes the oil? From little slicks left by passing ships, from giant slicks spreading over the oceans of the world, mixing with the flood of DDT washing from the continents.

Let us not weep for the birds only. The oxygen that supports animal life, including human life, is made by trees in forests and plankton in oceans. If we kill the plankton with oil and DDT, even as we kill the forests with urbanization, a time will come when we cannot breathe.

Man can walk on the Moon—and he can destroy oceans. The footsteps on the Moon may be our only epitaph after sludge worms have inherited the Earth.

A dying sea bird, wings gummed with oil, at Toleak Point. Who killed this bird, and who is killing the Pacific Ocean? The oil industry and all its customers—which is to say, all the people of the "civilized" world.